BASIC

BALLOON
SCULPTURE

Other Paragon-Reiss books include:

BASIC
BALLOON
SCULPTURE

George Schindler

ILLUSTRATED BY ALLISON ZAK,
LETTY AVELLAN, AND
ROSETTA FERRSON

Paragon-Reiss/New York

For Jack Rosa
who makes us smile
whenever he is near

Copyright George Schindler 1983

Library of Congress Cataloging in Publication Data

Schindler, George.
    Basic balloon sculpture.

    Bibliography: p.
    Includes index.
    1. Balloon sculpture.   I. Title.
TT926.S34   1983   736'.9   83-13474
ISBN 0-910199-01-9

Published by Paragon-Reiss Division, National Paragon Corporation,
57-07 31st Avenue, Woodside, N.Y. 11377

Contents

Foreword

It is indeed exciting to write the foreword to George Schindler's *Basic Balloon Sculpture*. I have known George for many years as a friend and fellow entertainer. His books on magic and ventriloquism have been teaching young people and hobbyists alike the basics of the art. This book is no exception.

Basic Balloon Sculpture is the first book, to my knowledge, that is offered to the public at large on the subject. Previous books and pamphlets have been written for magicians and clowns and have not been broadly circulated. Balloon sculpting is certainly an art and one that deserves recognition.

It was a great pleasure being able to teach George Schindler the basics of my "pinch and twist" method and I am happy that he is sharing it with you.

Jack Rosa

Preface

My introduction to the fascinating art of balloon modeling was by way of meeting a fellow magician whose name is Jack Rosa. Jack is an interesting man with many talents whose main pleasure in life is getting people to smile. His fast hands with a balloon always impressed me, and I never thought that someday I would not only be able to do this but write a book on the subject too. I soon learned that, in the hands of an artist, balloon sculpting is not as difficult as it first appears to be. No book on balloons should fail to recognize Joe La Monica. Joe, who makes his living as an entertainer, is probably one of the leading balloon workers in the country today. With friends like these, one has to be encouraged.

Balloon modeling is a recent addition to the American scene. There is no recorded history telling us who developed the techniques or when or where modeling started. In 1938, people first reported seeing balloon workers. Jay Marshall, a historian of the theater, recalls seeing Herbert Bonnert, of Pennsylvania, doing balloon sculptures at a magicians' convention in 1939.

As the "balloon act" developed, show people twisting several balloons into animal shapes became novelty acts. With their popularity came many ideas for new shapes and techniques. The first great balloon act I saw was that of John Shirley, who made numerous shapes of objects and animals from large balloons by twisting them together and adding an entertaining patter. John would close his act with his own creation—a balloon barrage in which hundreds of balloons were sent into a pleased audience.

The technique of modeling with a single balloon developed in the late 1960s with the publication of *One Balloon Zoo*, a book by Jimmy Davis. Pamphlets had already been written about large balloons, but now the "pencil balloon" came into its own. Davis's book triggered the "one-balloon revolution," which produced a series of books on balloon modeling. Balloon workers popped up everywhere, performing balloon acts. Magicians, clowns, and emcees took to carrying balloons in their pockets, eventually adding them to their shows. Today they can be seen on the streets, in shopping malls and restaurants, and in nightclub and theater acts.

The reason is simple: Sculpting balloons is both simple and fascinating. Once the basics are learned, you can acquire finesse through practice. The more you practice, the easier it will be for you to master the techniques and do different twists. You will soon be inventing creations of your own. Balloon sculpting isn't just for children to enjoy; everyone is fascinated by balloons. You will find that the adults in your audience will be the first to ask you for souvenirs to take home.

The sad part of balloon sculpting is that your artwork won't last forever. A well-inflated model will last about a week; others may vanish in a few hours, depending on the climate or the heat and humidity where you are working. When you have created that really great work of art, photograph it. Photographs are an impressive, long-lasting record of your balloon sculptures. For example, the balloon shapes shown on the cover of this book were sculpted by Robert Guida, a student of Jack Rosa.

Now let us go to work, so that you too can participate in the pleasure of making and decorating balloon sculptures.

Chapter 1

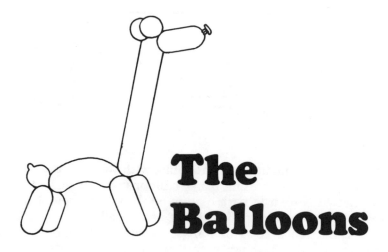

The Balloons

Balloon sculptors use a variety of balloons in their work. The sizes and shapes used depend on the size and type of sculptures they wish to create. We are going to work with simple, one-balloon shapes in which a standard "pencil balloon" is used. This balloon is long and thin and, as its name suggests, has a shape that resembles a pencil.

Pencil Balloons

The pencil balloon, or entertainer's balloon, is available in three different styles. The standard length is the easiest to blow up. When fully inflated, it measures about 2 inches in diameter by 45 inches long. When you have gained some experience modeling balloons, you can advance to the longer balloon, one measuring 2 inches in diameter but 60 inches long. Since this is a longer balloon, it will make larger animals and shapes. The longer balloon is made of a sturdier latex and will be somewhat harder to blow up.

It also comes in two styles. An even stronger latex is used by professional entertainers.

Almost all the shapes we will be working with in this book are made with pencil balloons (Figure 1). When you have learned how

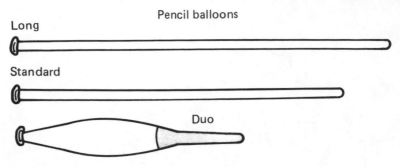

Figure 1

to use them, you can graduate to modeling with two or more balloons. I will offer help in using other balloons. Later on, when you have finished the basic part of this book, you can purchase other sizes to use in combination with the pencil balloon.

Balloons undergo a good deal of stress during the modeling process. They must be fresh when you start making your designs. Do not keep the balloons too long, or they will dry out. Store them loosely in a plastic bag in a cool, dry place. Avoid moisture or heat. Extreme hot or cold weather can ruin them. Do not crush the bag or the balloons will stick together. Balloons should last at least six months if you store them properly.

Although the factories take care to pack their balloons properly, you may occasionally find a flaw, such as a tiny hole. To avoid problems, it is important that you check your balloons carefully before working with them.

Blowing up the Balloons

The most difficult—and most important—part of making balloon sculptures is blowing up the balloon. Once mastered, the technique is quite simple, but it takes practice to learn. Be sure to take the time to learn this technique properly. Although balloon sculptors use pumps, you will find that your own breath offers the best warm air for the job.

The standard pencil balloon measures about nine inches when removed from its plastic bag. Stretching the balloon will add extra inches and make it easier to inflate. Hold the mouth end of the balloon in your left hand between the left thumb and index finger. This is the part you blow into. Take the tip, or nipple, end of the balloon in your right hand, holding it between the right thumb and index finger. Now separate your hands, stretching the balloon out as far as your arms will reach (Figure 2). This is not

← stretch →

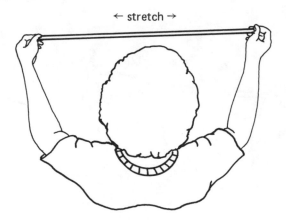

Figure 2

only good exercise, but if you do this three or four times before you start to blow, you will see that you have softened the rubber and have added about two inches to the balloon's length. Stop here and try this technique with several balloons—stretch three or four of them to prepare for the next step.

To inflate the balloon to its proper length, you will need to focus the air from your mouth so it enters the balloon in a smooth flow. Also, the stream of air must go into the tube without letting any escape outside. Blow into the balloon as though you were blowing through a straw, using the walls of your mouth to force the air out. Do not purse your lips or let your cheeks puff out. Your lips should be together except for the small space needed for the air to pass through. On your first try, you will need to blow only a small bubble of air into the balloon.

Hold the balloon in your left hand between the thumb and index finger. Take a deep breath, then bring it up to your mouth and place it between your lips. Use your right hand to help stretch the balloon a little by pulling at the tail. Pull the tail out a few inches. Blow the first stream of air into the balloon and stop, making sure no air escapes. You will have a small bubble of air caught at the top of the balloon (Figure 3).

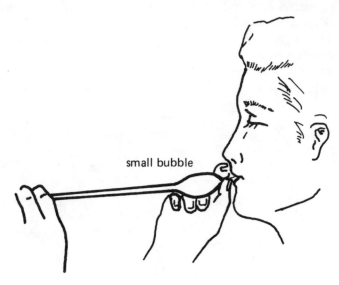

small bubble

Figure 3

Now take another deep breath. This time, blow air into the balloon in a long continuous stream from your chest cavity or your diaphragm. Do not allow your cheeks to puff out; merely blow while relaxing your thumb to open the tube. Be sure to keep a firm grip on the mouth of the balloon. Keep blowing until there is a long tube of air in the balloon. Do not blow it up fully, however; leave about five inches at the tail end (Figure 4). Pinch the nozzle to trap the air inside.

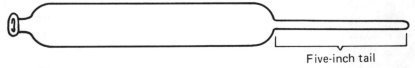

Five-inch tail

Figure 4

You have just completed the basic blowing procedure. Let the air out and repeat the procedure with the same balloon. It will be much easier the second time, since the balloon is now stretched and much softer. Use the same balloon for a third try, then repeat the procedure with a fresh balloon. After blowing up a few balloons you'll start to get the knack; and as you practice, the technique will become easier and easier.

Try the following aids if you are not successful at first.

* Cut a two-inch piece from the end of a plastic drinking straw.   After doing the initial stretching, insert half the straw in the nozzle of the balloon.   Leave about one inch sticking out of the balloon.   Be sure the edges of the straw are smooth so they won't puncture the latex of the balloon.   Try to blow up the balloon using the technique just described.   Blowing into the straw will give you the correct "feel."   It will also provide a firm support for your lips as you blow.

* Use good posture and breathe properly.   This will help you develop your chest muscles and make the technique easier. Stand up straight and take a few deep breaths before starting your balloon-blowing exercises.

* Practice moving your hands apart while stretching the balloon.

* Try blowing air out of your mouth, from your chest cavity, *without the balloon.*   Do this until you get a good flow.

* Hold a sheet of paper in front of you at arm's length.   Try to get the paper to move by blowing a steady stream of air at it, without puffing your cheeks.

A MOST IMPORTANT NOTE: As you are learning to blow up the balloons, try not to strain.   Do not allow the blowing to cause lightheadedness or a headache.

If you feel dizzy, STOP!   Relax—then try again a little later.   Avoid exertion.   If you feel any strain at all, *do not continue.*   By working too hard at the blowing stage, you could injure yourself.   Follow the recommended procedures for the best results.

While learning the knack, you may wish to blow up your balloons with a pump.   The easiest pump to use is a small bicycle pump.   It costs about three to four dollars and is operated with a small handle attached to one end. The other end has a plastic tube that serves as a nozzle for attaching pencil balloons. You might also consider a modified air-mattress pump, the type you can step on. For this type of pump, you will need a long tube attached to a nozzle.

A recent addition to the lineup of hand pumps available is the "Stevens" pump, named for Kathy Stevens, a clown who invented it. The Stevens pump can be carried in your pocket. It consists of a bulb that is squeezed with one hand. A small tube is fitted into a plastic nozzle. Some of the professional balloon dealers listed in the back of the book carry this type of pump (Figure 5).

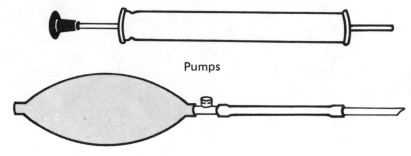

Pumps

Figure 5

If you develop a professional act later on, you may wish to purchase an electric compressor pump.

Tying the Knot

Once you have learned to inflate a balloon, you must learn to tie it so no air can escape. Follow the instructions given for blowing up balloons. Remember not to fill the balloon all the way—leave a five-inch tip at the end.

The balloon should be in your left hand, held by the left thumb and index finger. The nozzle end should be facing up. Relax the pressure of your thumb on the nozzle end, thus allowing some air to escape.

Use your right thumb and index finger to grasp the lip of the balloon. The lip is the small rolled-up part at the end of the nozzle (the part you blow into). Stretch the nozzle by pulling out the lip some four or five inches. Bring the lip around behind the left index finger, wrapping it around the index and middle fingers of your left hand (figures 6 and 7).

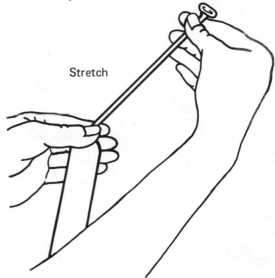

Stretch

Figure 6

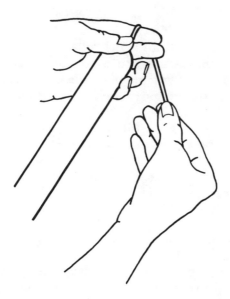

Figure 7

The stretched portion will crisscross the left index finger (Figure 8). Separate the left index and middle fingers. This will

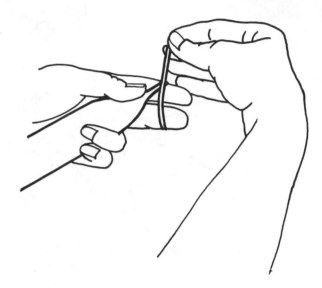

Figure 8

open a small space between the fingers. Using your *right* index finger, push the lip over the *left* index finger so it goes through the space. Your right thumb will hold the rolled end in place until you can get your right index finger to come around and take the end again. Gently ease your left index and middle fingers out of the loop. When you do this, a knot forms as air pressure locks the knot.

It makes no difference how the knot is tied. Some people like to roll the lip around the right index finger. Then they pull the finger back as they push the thumb forward. This pushes the lip through the small loop formed by the finger. Relaxing the left thumb causes the air pressure to form the knot. This, incidentally, is the way a tailor often ties a one-handed knot in a piece of thread.

Remember to allow a small amount of air to escape before starting to tie your knot. Keep a firm grip on the balloon as you do this so the balloon won't fly away by accident. It is also important to remember to leave extra inches at the end of the balloon. This provides space for the air to move into when you start making bubbles for your sculpture.

Chapter 2

Balloon Twists

            Once you have learned to blow up balloons and tie them in knots, you are ready to start learning to twist balloons into the various shapes needed to make simple animals. It is most important that you learn to handle inflated balloons without fear of breaking them. The pencil balloons used for modeling are made of sturdy latex and will not break easily. They are designed to withstand considerable punishment in handling. If you learn to relax as you do your bubble twists, you'll be successful and have loads of fun.

Basic Twist

Blow up your first balloon and tie a knot as you learned in Chapter 1. Be sure to leave four or five inches free of air in the tail section. Hold the tied balloon in your left hand with the knotted nozzle facing the ceiling and the tail pointing toward the floor. Rest the knot against the tip of your left index finger. Grasp the balloon with your right hand at a point just below the left pinky (Figure 9). Pinch the balloon between the right index finger and

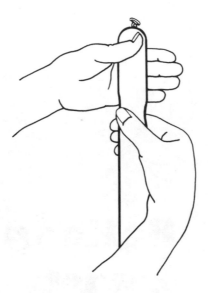

Figure 9

the thumb. While pinching your fingers together in this fashion, squeeze the balloon. A small amount of air will be transferred to the tail section. Now you can see why we left the tail end free of air.

Twist your right hand to the right, or counterclockwise. The part of the balloon still in your left hand is the "bubble." Continue to twist the lower part of the balloon with your right hand, turning it five or six times. This will lock the air in the bubble. *Always remember to twist the balloon AWAY FROM your body with your right hand*—your left hand will hold the bubbles in place as the right hand does the work. This method of twisting, called the "pinch and twist," is used by the balloon sculptor Jack Rosa. Slide your left fingers down along the bubble until your left thumb and index finger meet at the twisted section. With your left finger and thumb, hold the bubble in place while you hold the remainder of the balloon with your other fingers. Your right hand is now free to continue with the next step.

Second and Third Bubbles

Your left hand holds the balloon as you grasp it with your right hand just below the left pinky (Figure 10). Pinch the balloon at

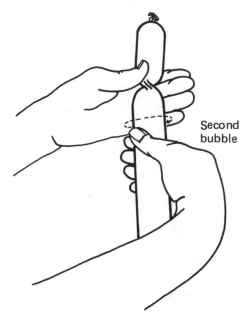

Second
bubble

Figure 10

this point as you did in forming the Basic Twist. Do this with your right thumb and right index finger. Twist the second section to the right, continuing to twist four or five times and locking off another bubble. You now have two bubbles in your left hand. If you wrap your left fingers around the second bubble, both bubbles will be held in place with one hand.

    With your free hand, bring the rest of the balloon up alongside the two bubbles (Figure 11). Open your left hand so the fingers can encircle the lower half of the balloon. Slide your index finger between the bubbles at the twisted section, as shown in Figure 11. By pinching your left index and middle fingers together, you can make a third bubble. With your right hand, twist this bubble and lock it as follows: Your right thumb should be on top, and your right fingers should be under the section marked x (Figure 12). Roll the right thumb to your left as your right middle finger rolls away to your right. Do this four or five times; this twists the section and locks it. Use your left middle finger to hold the three bubbles together in the crotch of your thumb. The right hand is now free.

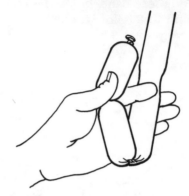

Figure 11

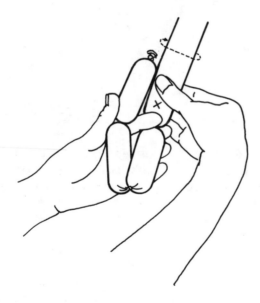

Figure 12

Lock Twist

Figure 13 shows the right hand holding the two bottom bubbles.

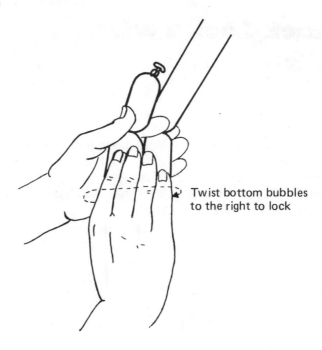

Twist bottom bubbles
to the right to lock

Figure 13

Four fingers are on top, and the thumb is underneath. Twist both
bubbles to your right a few times. This locks the bubbles in place.
Now both your hands are free again. Three bubbles are needed to
form the Lock Twist. (Figure 14).

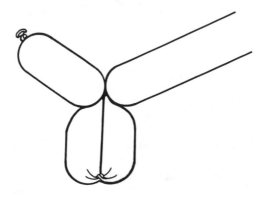

Figure 14

Quick-Lock Twist

The Quick-Lock Twist is a shortcut in twisting and locking bubbles. The twist does not give you clearly defined bubbles, but in many ways it serves the purpose, as you will see later.

To make the Quick-Lock Twist, hold an inflated balloon in your left hand with the tail pointing toward the floor and the nozzle toward the ceiling. Your left thumb should be about three inches from the formed knot. Fold the bottom of the balloon upward so it creases exactly at your left pinky. The tail half is now pointed at the ceiling, and your left hand is holding the folded balloon (Figure 15).

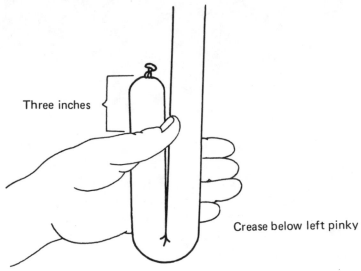

Three inches

Crease below left pinky

Figure 15

Move the balloon down so that the knot is now an inch from your left thumb. With your free, right hand, twist both sections under the left pinky. *Always twist to the right, away from your body.* To lock the twist, twist the balloon four or five times. In one twist you have made a similar model. The difference is that the bubbles are not clearly individual.

The Quick-Lock Twist is often used by clowns and many birthday-party performers who have to make many models for giveaways and therefore must work faster (figures 16 and 17).

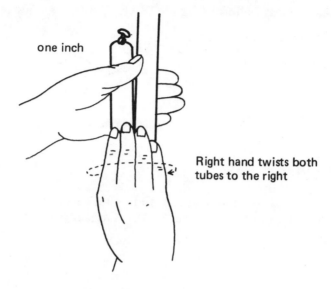

one inch

Right hand twists both
tubes to the right

Figure 16

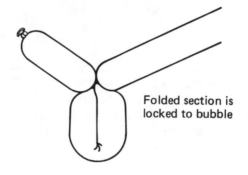

Folded section is
locked to bubble

Figure 17

Apple Twist

The Apple Twist is an unusual shape to use in making your first
bubble. After you have tied the knot, hold the balloon horizontally
so the knot is facing to your right. The tail is at your left. The
left hand should be positioned about three inches from the knot
end. With your right index finger, push the knot into the soft

center of your balloon (Figure 18A). While the knot is inside the

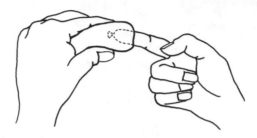

Figure 18 A

balloon, your left index finger and thumb should pinch it so that,
it remains in place (Figure 18B). Carefully remove your right

Figure 18 B

finger while holding the knot tightly with your left hand. Your
right hand is now free to twist a bubble in front of the left fingers.
Turn the bubble counterclockwise (away from you) three or four
times. This will lock the knot inside the balloon. The bubble will
then have a flat, dimpled look (Figure 18C).

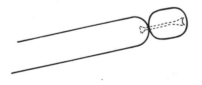

Figure 18 C

The name of this twist comes from its use in shaping an apple
with a smaller duo balloon. We'll cover this is Chapter 6 when we
make Apples for our fruit basket. In the meantime, work on this
twist since we will use it later for an animal balloon.

Chapter 3

Basic Dog

Most of the animals we will be making with a simple pencil balloon require ten bubbles and three lock twists. The proportions, or sizes, of the bubbles will vary. The length of the tail will change from animal to animal, but the basic twists we have already learned will be very much like the Basic Dog. Learn this one, and you can do all the rest merely by altering some of their proportions.

Start your Basic Dog by blowing up a pencil balloon, leaving a five-inch tail. Let out a bit of air and tie the knot you have already learned. You do not need a ruler to measure the five inches. As you progress, you will be able to estimate various lengths from experience. Your eye will tell you when the tail, or bubble, is too long or too short. The first time or two, estimate five inches and then check it with a ruler.

The nose and ears of your dog will be the same size. Each bubble you make will be the same size as the nose and the ears. Use your fingers to measure the size of the bubble. The bottom of your left pinky can be used as a guide to judge the distance. If you wish to make smaller bubbles, do the first twist by measuring your bubble against the ring (or fourth) finger. Move your pinky out of the way (Figure 19).

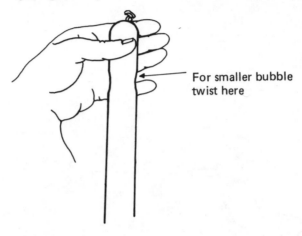

For smaller bubble twist here

Figure 19

Decide whether to use three or four fingers. Then twist your first bubble to that size. *Remember to twist away from your body.* Hold the first bubble between the left index finger and thumb at the twist. Measure the next bubble with your fingers and twist

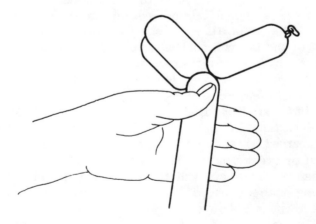

Figure 20

again. The second bubble should be the same size as the first. Twist the second and third bubbles and lock them with the Lock Twist.

Turn the balloon so that the tail faces the floor. Now look at it. The bubble with the knot at the end represents the dog's nose; the other two bubbles are its ears. Hold the balloon between the left thumb and index finger just below the bubbles (Figure 20). Pretend the first three bubbles do not exist. Start at this point as though you were using a fresh balloon. Twist three more bubbles all the same size as before. Measure the same distance, using your fingers as a guide. The next bubble you make will be the dog's neck (Figure 21). Twist bubbles numbers two and three as before

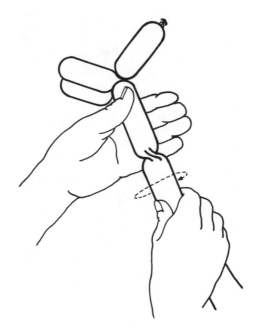

Figure 21

and lock them as you did earlier (figures 22 and 23). Your dog now has a neck and two front legs (Figure 24).

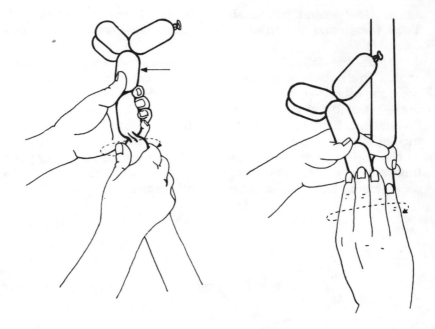

Figure 22   Figure 23

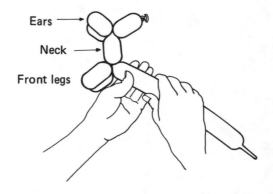

Ears
Neck
Front legs

Figure 24

Position your hands as in **Figure 24** and start the series of twists all over again (figures 25 and 26). This time you will find

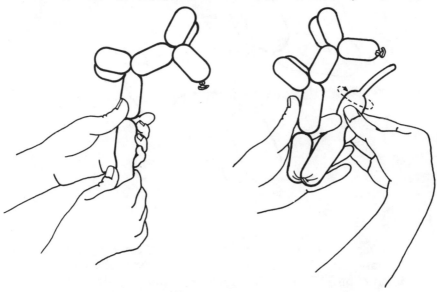

Figure 25   Figure 26

that there does not seem to be much balloon left to work with. As you twist each new bubble you will see why we left a long tail. Every time you twist a bubble, more air flows into the tail, making it shorter. You'll have just enough air left to lock the three new bubbles. These will become the body and the hind legs of your dog. Be sure to keep the last set of bubbles the same size as the earlier ones. The remainder of the balloon's tail will become the cute tail of your dog. Adjust the bubbles so the dog's nose and ears are straight and so both legs face in the same direction.

The tail will stand straight up in the air (Figure 27).

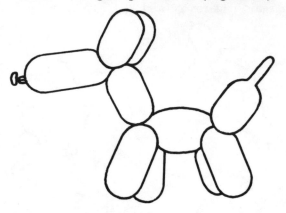

Figure 27

To make the dog more realistic, draw some eyes or lashes on the nose part. (See Chapter 7, "Drawing Faces and Highlights," for instruction.) Figure 28, shows the summary structure of the Basic Dog.

Nose   Ears   Neck Front legs Body Rear legs Tail

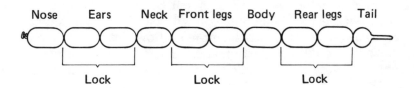

Lock   Lock   Lock

Figure 28

Chapter 4

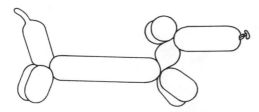

The Animals

Now that you have seen how easy it is to make the Basic Dog, you should be encouraged to try other animals. You will see that you need to make only a few adjustments to capture the characteristics of other animals. A perfect example of applying a simple change is in the making of the Poodle.

Poodle

Follow the instructions for sculpting the Basic Dog. Be sure all the bubbles are the same size. Hold the finished dog in front of you and turn its head so the head and ears face the tail. Your dog is now looking back at you.

Hold the animal by the ears, positioning the fingers of both hands behind the ears (Figure 29). Use your right thumb to push the bottom of the nose bubble up toward the top twist of the ears. Both thumbs now hold the nose in place as your fingers roll the ears in toward the nose. Roll the ears with an even pressure.

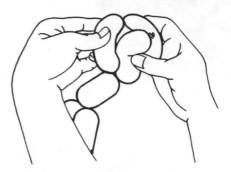

Figure 29

Do *not* push the nose, but instead allow the ears to move inward. The nose will fill the space; but allow it to go only *halfway* into this space. The nose should stay locked in place by the pressure of the air on the ear bubbles. Adjust the ears and nose so they face forward again. You have now given the dog a cute poodle hairstyle (Figure 30). But you are not finished.

Figure 30

With your right index finger and thumb, pinch the uninflated part of the tail at the point where it meets the bubble. Hold this place firmly as your left index finger and thumb pull the tail out, stretching it as far as it will go. Allow the tail to snap back in place like a rubber band (figures 31A and 31B). By squeezing the tail bubble with the right fingers, you will cause a small bubble to appear at the tip of the tail (Figure 31B). This pom-pom tip completes your Poodle (Figure 32).

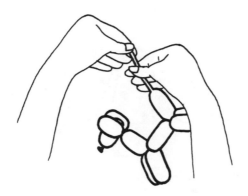

Figure 31 A

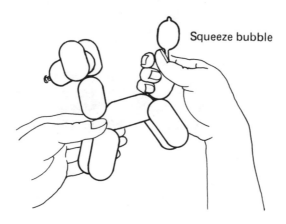

Squeeze bubble

Figure 31 B

Figure 32

Dachshund

We have learned that by adjusting the bubbles or pinching the tail we can alter the Basic Dog to look like a poodle. Other animals require other changes. The Dachshund, a long little doggie, is made the same way as the Basic Dog, but the size of the bubbles varies. This is the way we do it.

Inflate your balloon. Let out a small amount of air and tie off the balloon as before. Leave a four- or five-inch tail. Make your first bubble about three inches long. If you measure with your fingers, position the balloon at a point about the width of three fingers for your first twist. The ear twists should be about half the size of the initial nose twist. Make the bubbles about an inch and a half long. Twist and lock them (Figure 33).

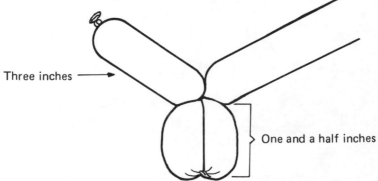

Three inches ⟶

One and a half inches

Figure 33

Make the neck bubble about the same as the ears—approximately an inch and half. The two legs can be a bit longer than the neck, say about two inches long.

Up to this point, you have followed the basic procedure used in making the Basic Dog. Here is where you will change the style.

Turn the balloon around. The tail end is up where you usually have the knotted end. Twist a three-inch bubble from this end, as though it were a nose (Figure 34). Twist two more ear bubbles

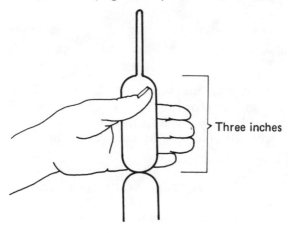

Three inches

Figure 34

about two inches long and lock them together. You will have a long bubble in the center that acts as the body. Turn the animal

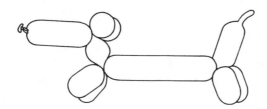

Figure 35

around and adjust it. The knot will be the nose of your dog and the uninflated tip will be its tail. A few marks with a felt-tip marking pen (see Chapter 6), and you'll have a cute Dachshund (Figure 35). A summary sketch is shown in Figure 36.

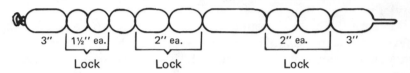

3″   1½″ ea.   2″ ea.   2″ ea.   3″
Lock   Lock   Lock

Figure 36

Giraffe

You may wonder why the Giraffe follows the dogs in our sequence of balloon sculptures. The answer is simple. The Giraffe is made very much in the same manner as the Basic Dog or the Dachshund. The difference is in the proportions of the bubbles being twisted.

Actually, the ears of our Giraffe are much like little horns. The Giraffe's neck is quite long, and its body arches upward. To capture the way a giraffe looks, we make the two front legs a little longer than the hind legs. Here is how to make the Giraffe.

When you inflate your balloon, leave only a two-inch tail before tying the knot. You will need more length for this character. An orange balloon makes a nice-looking Giraffe.

Twist the first bubble at a length of about two and a half inches. This is the nose section. Make the next two bubbles only one inch long; then lock them (Figure 37A—Step 1).

The neck will be a long bubble eight or nine inches long. Twist this bubble, then make the two front legs about four inches long. Lock the three bubbles together (Figure 37B—Step 2).

The body length will depend on the amount of air left over; so turn the figure around as you did with the Dachshund and make a small bubble tail and two hind legs, each one two or three inches long. When you lock these three bubbles, the body will form between the front and rear legs (Figure 37C—Step 3). Your

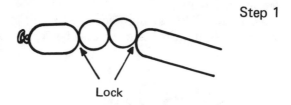

Step 1

Lock

Figure 37 A

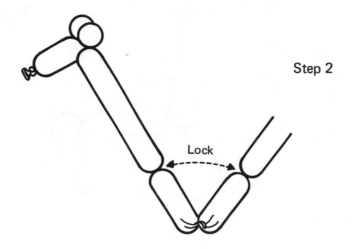

Step 2

Lock

Figure 37 B

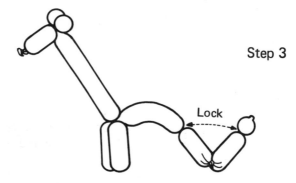

Step 3

Lock

Figure 37 C

completed animal should look like Figure 38. A summary sketch is shown in Figure 39.

See Chapter 7, "Drawing Faces and Highlights"; with some irregular circles drawn on his neck and back, this fellow can really be handsome.

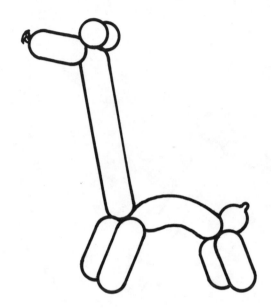

Figure 38

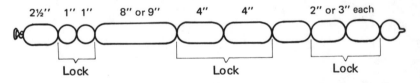

| 2½" | 1" 1" | 8" or 9" | 4" | 4" | | 2" or 3" each | | |

Lock   Lock   Lock

Figure 39

Rabbit

Once again, we will change a few bubble sizes. This time our animal will be sitting down. A white or yellow balloon makes a nice-looking bunny.

Inflate your balloon, leaving a three-inch tail. Just as a reminder, always let out a small amount of air from the balloon before tying it off. Twist the nose with a small bubble about an inch and a half long. The Rabbit ears must be fairly large, so make each one about three inches. Lock the bubbles. The neck will be very tiny. Twist a half-inch bubble. Make each of the two front-leg bubbles three inches long. Lock the neck and paws together.

The body, or back, of the Rabbit should be about three inches in length. Twist this bubble, but hold it firmly between the index finger and the thumb. With your right hand twist a small bubble from the tail end—this bubble should be about an inch and a half (Figure 40 C). Continue to hold the body with your left hand

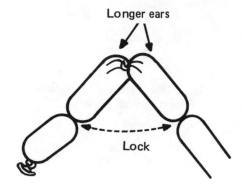

Figure 40 A

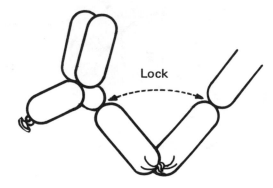

Figure 40 B

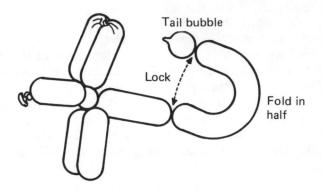

Figure 40 C

Fold the bottom of the balloon up to meet the body. The tail bubble and the body bubble should be locked together by the Quick-Lock Twist. (We described this twist in Chapter 2.) This forms a circle at the bottom of your sculpture (figures 41 and 42).

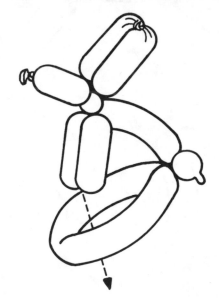

Figure 41

Bring the two front legs down and set them in the circle. The latex itself will lock the legs in place. Set the Rabbit on a table. The

Figure 42

circle becomes a base that will prevent it from falling down. Adjust the ears on your sitting Rabbit and dress it up by using a felt marking pen. A summary sketch is shown in Figure 43.

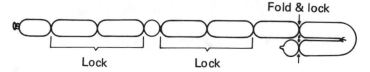

Figure 43

Mouse

Since our Mouse sculpture will be very small, the bubbles naturally will have to be tiny. I recommend that you blow up your balloon so that there are only ten inches of air, leaving the rest of the tail uninflated. Release a small amount of air before tying the knot (Figure 44).

Figure 44

Each bubble you make must be the same as the others. A one-inch bubble is just right for the purpose. It will also give you practice in making small bubbles for fancier animals when you get to the more advanced stage of the art.

The Mouse is made exactly like the Basic Dog. The differences are only in the size of the bubbles and the length of the tail, differences that give the little Mouse its charm.

Follow all the instructions for the Basic Dog, and you will have the Mouse (Figure 45).

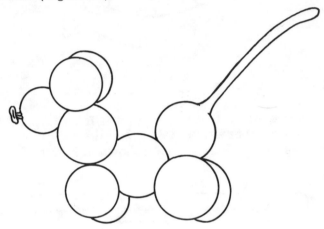

Figure 45

Dobbin the Horse

We will learn a new twist for the balloon sculpture Dobbin the Horse. Leave a three-inch tail on your balloon when you blow it up for Dobbin. Allow a small amount of air to escape as usual and tie the balloon in the usual manner. Start by twisting your first bubble, making it three and a half inches in length.

Make another bubble two inches long—this will be the ear bubble. Hold this bubble in place with your left hand, as you did with the sculptures already described. This time, before making another bubble, bring the bottom of the balloon up so the tip points at the ceiling (Figure 46A). Move the bubble up so that the twists line up as shown in the figure. With your left hand, hold both sides of the balloon firmly.

Grasp the ear bubble with your right hand. Pull and twist at the same time to lock this small ear in place (Figure 46B). Repeat this procedure with another two-inch bubble. Now you have the second ear.

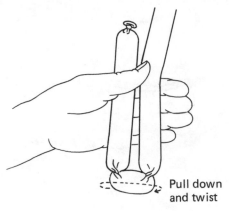

Figure 46 A

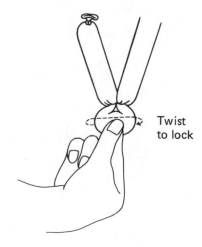

Figure 46 B

Hold the balloon in your left hand again, as shown in Figure 47. With your left thumb, push the bubble against the side of the balloon under the ears; the other four fingers hold the balloon in place. Both sides of the balloon are secured by slipping a small loosely fitting rubber band around them, as shown in Figure 47. The rubber band should hold the bubbles together without too much pressure.

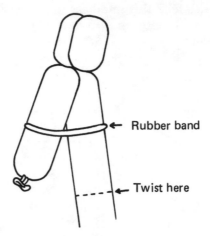

Figure 47

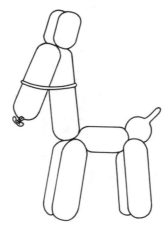

Figure 48

Make your next twist about an inch longer than the head. Twist as indicated by the broken line in Figure 47. This gives you the proper proportions. Twist two more three-inch bubbles for the front legs. The body should be two inches long and each hind leg three inches (Figure 48).

The famous balloon sculptor Joe La Monica originated the idea of adding reins to the horse. Instead of a rubber band, he uses another pencil balloon and actually ties a loop around the nose and then the neck. La Monica suggests using a discarded pencil balloon, one that popped or is torn, so you won't waste the pieces.

Hobbyhorse

You can dress the horse sculpture by adding another balloon and making a base to create your Hobbyhorse. Blow up another pencil

—— Halfway point

Figure 49

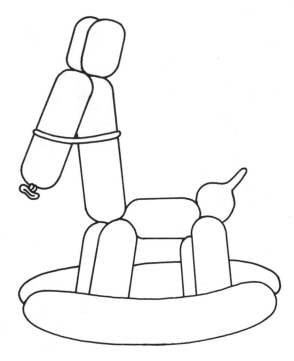

Figure 50

balloon, leaving a five-inch tip. Bring the tail up to meet the knot. Crisscross the ends so that the knot meets the tail at the end of the inflated part (Figure 49). The balloon is folded in half. Twist the balloon at the halfway point where it is creased. Twist it a few times. Now, tie the nozzle end to the tail end, using a standard knot. This is the type of knot you might use when tying something with string. Make a double knot and tie it securely. You can now cut off the excess tip. If the knot is really tight, you can actually snap off the tip by stretching it away from the balloon.

You have two tubes tied at one end and twisted on the other. Set the Hobbyhorse in the base with the legs locked against the sides (Figure 50). If the tubes are too long, Quick-Lock Twist a bubble at either or both ends.

Easy Dog

Many balloon sculptors do not have the time to spend on individual bubbles because they must make lots of balloons the fastest way possible. While the features are not detailed, they can still be made to represent the animal. Here is an example of what I call the "Easy Dog."

Blow up your balloon in the prescribed manner, leaving a five-inch tail. Let out a small amount of air before you tie the knot. (Refer to the section "Quick-Lock Twist" in Chapter 2.)

Fold the balloon so that it creases at about one fourth of the way down from the knot. Hold the balloon firmly between the left thumb and fingers and Quick-Lock Twist both sides to form the first bubble. This twist is made about halfway between the knot and the crease (Figure 51).

Use your eye to estimate the distance between the lock and the point where the tail begins. Fold the balloon so that it creases at about one third of this distance. Hold the balloon firmly, as before, and twist the two sides in half, using the Quick-Lock Twist. This twist is used to form the body and front legs of your animal.

Bend the tail back to meet the last twist. Twist the hind legs at a point one third of the length of the folded tube. If you pinch the tail between your left thumb and index finger, the air will not flow into the tail too quickly. Your dog is now complete (Figure 52).

You will find that, although the bubbles are not in exact proportion, the sculpture still looks like a dog. Draw the face and eyes to finish the job (see Chapter 7).

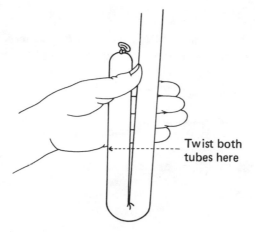

Figure 51

Figure 52

Easy Poodle

The Easy Dog can easily be converted into a poodle. The procedure is just like that for the regular poodle: You must fit the nose into the open space formed by the ears. Follow the same steps shown in Figure 29. Make sure to roll the ears around the nose so that it sits halfway in the loop. Pinch the tail as you did for the regular poodle. The decorations on the face will make the difference and offer more character to this sculpture.

Swan

The Swan, one of the prettiest of the balloon sculptures, is quite simple to make. The flowing curve of the neck and the expressive eyes you will draw give this sculpture its character. For the best results, choose a white balloon or a light-colored one, such as pink or yellow.

Blow up your balloon in the regular manner, leaving only a two-inch tip. As you blow it up, stretch the balloon a bit to make a long, thin tube.

Make your first twist at a point about 12 inches from the tail end (Figure 53). Twist it four or five times to lock the long

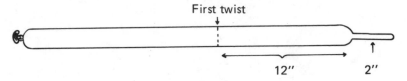

Figure 53

bubble in place. Secure the twist between the left fingers and the thumb. Use your right hand to bring the knot up to meet the twisted section. Now tie the knot to the twist, forming a ring (Figure 54). You can wrap the end of the knot around the twist, but it is better to stretch the rubber at the knot and tie it in.

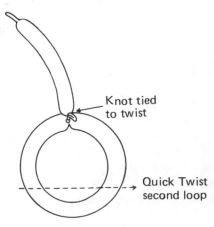

Figure 54

Gently squeeze the bottom of the circle. This will allow you to twist both sides in a two- or three-inch bubble, using the Quick-Lock Twist. This will form another loop (Figure 55). The tail end

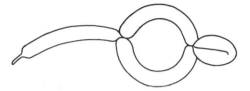

Figure 55

of the balloon becomes the Swan's beak. Hold the balloon by the tip of the tail. Your left thumb should press the short tail against the inside of the index and middle fingers of your left hand (Figure 56A). Turn your wrist downward. Use your right hand to wrap the balloon around the fingers of your left hand a few times (Figure 56B). This forms a coil. Hold the rolled balloon with the

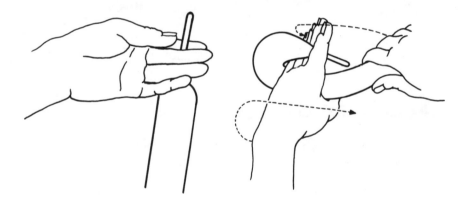

Figure 56 A   Figure 56 B

left hand and bring it up to your mouth. Breathe against the rolled side of the coil giving it some warmth. Release your left fingers and allow the balloon to unroll. Note how the shape now looks like a swan's neck.

  Bring the bottom of the neck down to meet the first twist

and secure it against the sides of the base. If you gently squeeze the balloon about two inches from the beak, the end will puff out slightly to look more like a head (Figure 57). You are now ready to decorate your work.

Figure 57

Another Swan

Begin this design by blowing up a balloon as before, leaving a two-inch tail. Your first twist should be a one-inch bubble at the tied end. Hold this bubble at the twist between the left thumb and index finger. Fold the remaining portion of the balloon in half and bring it up alongside the bubble. Pinch the tube at the half-way point between the left index and middle fingers (Figure 58). With your right hand, twist the tube to the right as you did in the third bubble of the Basic Dog. Once this is done, lock the small bubble to the new twist, thus forming a large circle. Grasp the tie and wrap it around the fingers as you did with the first Swan (Figure 56). Breathe some air into the coiled portion before you let it unroll. Adjust the Swan's head as before. The smaller bubble should be in front of the Swan. Tuck the base of the Swan's neck into the opening at the twist adjoining the small

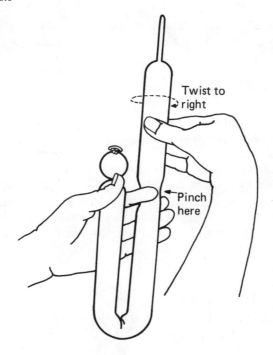

Twist to
right

Pinch
here

Figure 58

Figure 59

bubble (Figure 59). A long pencil balloon makes an excellent Swan hat. (See Chapter 6, section on "Balloon Hats.")

Polly Parrot

Polly Parrot is a bit more difficult, but once you master the handling you can make more difficult sculptures with ease. Inflate a balloon, leaving a two-inch tip. Let a small amount of air out before you tie the knot. Make your first bubble about an inch and a half long. Make two more bubbles, each about two inches, and lock all three bubbles together. Here is how to form the Parrot's head. Grasp the knot and stretch it over the top of the other two bubbles. Tuck it under the twist. Push the knot between the two head bubbles so it is out of sight (Figure 60). This becomes the Parrot's beak.

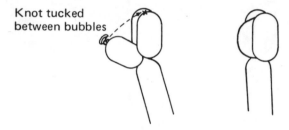

Knot tucked
between bubbles

Figure 60

The next series of bubbles requires some work on your part. Make a one-inch bubble and twist it five or six times. Hold it in place by locking it in the crotch formed by your left thumb and index finger. The next bubble should be five inches long. Twist it securely. The bubble should stay in place as your left index and middle fingers pinch a one-inch bubble. Your left hand holds the balloon while your right hand makes all the twists. Once you have the small bubble, the left ring finger pushes it to the side so that your left index and middle fingers can pinch another one-inch bubble. Twist all the bubbles securely. All the left fingers hold the bubbles in place as the right hand twists a five-inch bubble. Open your left hand so that all four bubbles are held in the palm (Figure 61). With your right hand, lock the two five-inch bubbles together.

The small, bottom bubbles represent the Parrot's feet. The

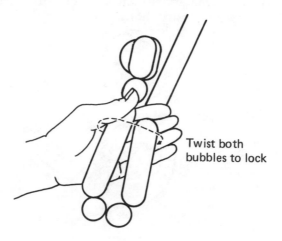

Figure 61

five-inch sides become the wings. Squeeze all the air into the tail of the remaining tube and push this tube halfway into the opening above the feet (Figure 62). This will make Polly's long tail. Here,

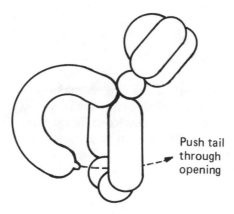

Push tail through opening

Figure 62

the decorations are important. Design the bird with your felt marking pen, making a prominent beak, nice feathers on the tail and the wings, and large visible eyes on the sides of the head

(Figure 63). A summary sketch is shown in Figure 64. See Chapter 7 for marking instructions.

Figure 63

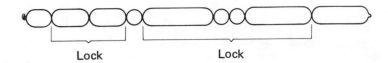

Lock   Lock

Figure 64

Bumblebee

Here is an easy balloon sculpture to make. Blow up your pencil balloon, leaving a one-and-one-half-inch tip. Remember to release a little air before you tie your knot. Make the first twist an inch and a half from the knot—hold it in place with your thumb and index finger. Bring the bottom of the balloon up and make another twist about five inches from the tail end. Lock this twist to the first one (Figure 65). From this point *(x)*, estimate the halfway point around the circle you just formed *(y)*. Pinch this halfway point at the bottom to the *x* at the top of the circle and squeeze them into the twist. This forms two wings. Twist one of the wings around into the bubbles to lock it in place. The Bumblebee's head will be the section with the knot at its nose; the tail

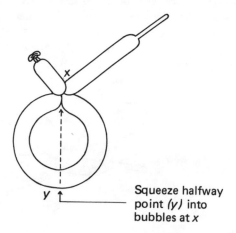

Squeeze halfway
point *(y)* into
bubbles at *x*

Figure 65

section is at the opposite end under the wings (Figure 66). Adjust the sections so the wings are on the sides of the head. Dress the body by drawing thick, black connecting lines all around the bubble. Make two small eyes on its head and perhaps a smile on the face.

Figure 66

Hummingbird

This is made almost exactly as you made the Bumblebee. Leave a two-inch tip at the end of a balloon. Twist the knot section into a four-inch tail. Make the tail section two inches and lock the sections together. This is the opposite of the way you made the

Bumblebee. Once the bubbles are locked, estimate the midpoint of the loop, then squeeze it into the head-and-body section. This time you will see that the bird's head is the pointy tail end of the balloon. The body is the part with the knot. Draw a pair of small eyes near the needle nose (Figure 67).

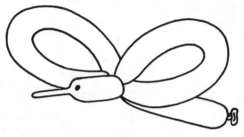

Figure 67

Chapter 5

Multiple Balloon Models

A great variety of shapes and forms can be made with balloons by combining more than one of a single type or by adding several balloons of different sizes. Here are several examples of sculptures made with more than one balloon.

Octopus

The Octopus is a great sculpture for use as a decoration and as a fun giveaway animal. It is made with four regular pencil balloons. Select four different colors for a flashier creature. Blow up all four balloons, leaving the smallest possible tip—perhaps only a quarter inch. Try to make each balloon the same length, which will give you four long tubes. Hold the tubes together in close alignment, tips pointed toward the floor and knots toward the ceiling. Grasp the balloons with your left hand at about the center of the bunch. Use your right hand to twist the four balloons with a single turn. The result is eight spokes coming out of the center of the twist (Figure 68).

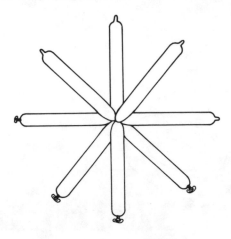

Figure 68

Bring all the ends together with your right hand so the ends are facing the floor. Hold them in your left hand about six inches from the twist. Use your right hand to twist all eight ends at once. Don't be intimidated by the number of balloons; the latex is sturdy enough to take the twists. The end result is seen in figures 69 and 70.

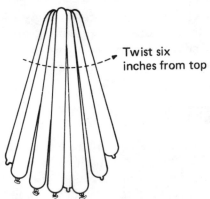

Twist six
inches from top

Figure 69

Figure 70

Your creation can be decorated by drawing large eyes that resemble those of an octopus. On the other hand, if you use a dark-colored balloon for all four lengths, your figure can be made to resemble a large spider.

"Texas" Bumblebee

We have already seen that the longer pencil balloons make larger animals. For the "Texas" Bumblebee you can use a regular pencil balloon, but a longer one is better. You will also need a duo balloon. The duo balloon is a small balloon made in a two-color design with a small, pointed tip about an inch and a half long. The rest of the

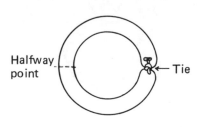

Figure 71 A   Figure 71 B

balloon is about three inches long. This type of balloon can be blown up to 21 inches if necessary. The tip is usually a darker, contrasting color. The duo balloon is a versatile balloon, as you will see. This sculpture uses two balloons, a regular and a duo.

Blow up a pencil balloon. If you use a longer balloon, you'll need more air. Allow only about half an inch for the tip and tie it off. Make a figure-eight design as follows. First, tie the tip to the knot end with a regular knot, as you would tie a piece of string. A continuous loop will be formed. Locate the halfway point of the loop directly across from the knot (Figure 71A). Bring this

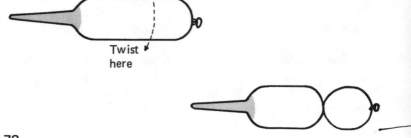

Twist
here

Figure 72

Figure 73

point to the knot and twist both tubes, locking them together (Figure 71B). Tuck the figure eight under your arm for use in a moment.

Blow up the duo balloon as follows: Fill the balloon with air only up to the point where the tip changes color. Stop here and tie a regular knot. Twist the balloon two thirds of the way between the tip and the knot (Figure 72). Lock this twist into the twist of the figure eight under your arm. One twist will do. You now have a lovely bumblebee. The knot is its nose and the tail has a unique point. If you use a yellow duo balloon, draw black lines around the body to make it look more realistic (Figure 73).

Another Hummingbird

You may have already guessed that the Bumblebee can be easily transformed into the Hummingbird. Make the sculpture as you did the "Texas" Bumblebee except for the nose. This time, the needle point of the duo balloon serves as the nose, and the two-thirds twist is toward the knot. The knot becomes the tail, and the pointed section forms the nose.

Parrot on a Swing

This character makes an excellent hanging decoration for a party. Although you can make a Parrot on a Swing with a regular pencil balloon, I suggest an extra long one if it is available, so that it will provide a larger swing for your parrot. This is the way to make it.

Blow up your balloon, leaving a two-inch tip. Let out a small amount of air and tie the balloon. Once it is at its maximum length, carefully push your right index finger into the balloon, pushing the knot in about two inches. This is just like the Apple Twist mentioned in Chapter 2. Extreme care must be taken, however, so as not to puncture the balloon with your fingernail. Use your left thumb and index finger to pinch the knot from the outside, holding it in place. *Gently* ease your finger out of the balloon. Do not pull it out quickly. Once you have removed your finger, twist a bubble at that point. Your right fingers should rotate the bubble about a dozen times; this will ensure that it is properly locked (Figure 74).

Form a loop by bringing the tip end of the balloon across the

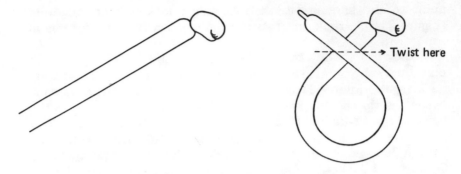

Figure 74   Figure 75

bubble end, as shown in Figure 75. The two ends should cross
about two inches from the bubble. Three inches of the tail should
overlap this loop. At point x, give both sections a Quick-Lock Twist
to lock them together (Figure 76). Bring the tip end into the center

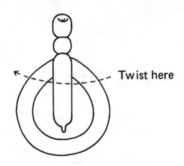

Figure 76

Figure 77

of the loop and Quick-Lock Twist all three sections together (Figure 77). Once you have done this, gently push all the bubbles through the center of the loop so they come out the other side to form a parrot sitting on its perch.

If you wish to hang Parrot on a Swing as a display, tie a small loop of an unused balloon around the top halfway point on the swing. Tie it loosely so there is no pressure on the tube. The other end of the unused balloon can be tied with a string for hanging. (Note: When a balloon breaks, save the loose rubber piece. It makes excellent string for tying ribbons or hanging balloons.)

The Parrot on a Swing can be decorated with bright colors.

Penguin

Here is a cute little animal that is made with a duo balloon.

It is ideal for use as a place card at a party. The Penguin was developed by Mark Schwartzberg, a New York balloon worker.

Blow up your duo balloon so that only the main body is filled. Do not allow air into the pointed tip. Tie a knot in the base of the balloon and hold it in your left hand. Use your right index finger and thumb to pull down the colored tip at the point where the two colors meet. Pull the tip down so it touches the bottom knot (Figure 78A). As you do this, squeeze the center of the bal-

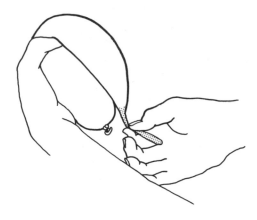

Figure 78 A

loon *gently* with your left hand. Repeat this procedure several times, and you will find that the balloon takes the shape of a Penguin. The drawings you will add to this figure are important and will complete the character.

Use a 3-by-5 card as a place card. Punch two small pencil holes in the card about an inch from the shorter side of the card. Push the knot into the first hole x and bring it back up through the second hole y. In this way, the Penguin stands by itself (Figure 78B). It should face the opposite end of the card so a child's name can be drawn on the remaining white surface and used as a place card. You can use other colors for additional place cards to decorate your party table. In a pinch, use a playing card or a business card as a stand, though the index card makes a better base.

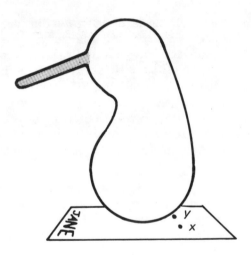

Figure 78 B

Chapter 6

Decorating with Balloons

There is nothing more colorful than balloon sculptures for party decorations. In addition to a few animals that can be hanging or displayed around the room, you can make place cards or centerpiece decorations for your table. The Penguin is an example. Parrot on a Swing is another. The sculptures described below are examples of what you can do to brighten up a party table. Use your imagination to vary the sculptures.

Fruit Basket

In addition to being a colorful table centerpiece, this basket makes a lovely gift for someone in the hospital. Whereas candy and flowers do not last, a balloon Fruit Basket can last for days. It is bright, cheerful, and nonfattening.

You will need three pencil balloons of the same color for the basket. Use regular-size balloons for the base and an extra-long balloon for the handle. White is a good color to use to show off the contents.

Inflate the two regular balloons so they are about the same size. Leave a quarter-inch tip, which will be used to tie the ends together later. Find the midpoint of the first balloon. You can do this by touching the tip to the knot. The tube will increase at the midpoint. Twist the balloon at this midpoint and give it two or three turns. Now tie the loose tip to the knot. You now have an oval formed by the tubes. Do the same with the second balloon. The two ovals should be the same size.

Lay one oval flat on the table. Turn the second oval so the tubes are in a horizontal position. Insert the oval into the center of the oval on the table. Lift the balloons off the table as you work. Wrap the knot on the second balloon around the twisted end of the first balloon. Do the same on the other end, wrapping the knot of the bottom balloon into the twisted section of the second oval (Figure 79). The result is a football-shaped mass con-

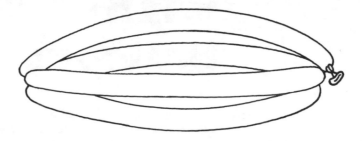

Figure 79

sisting of four tubes. If you set this on a table, it will stand by it-self, supported by the two bottom tubes. The balloons, locked in place by the twisted knots, will stay together. This is the cradle. You now need a handle for the basket.

Inflate the longer balloon. If one is not available, the regular size will do (but it will make a shorter handle). Leave a one-inch tip, let out some air, and tie it off.

Twist a one-inch bubble in the knot end of the tube. After giving it a few turns, wrap the twisted portion around one end of the cradle, where the knots join. Twist another bubble on the tip end of the handle. Wrap this bubble around the other end of the cradle. A few twists will lock it in place, and you have a finished basket (Figure 80).

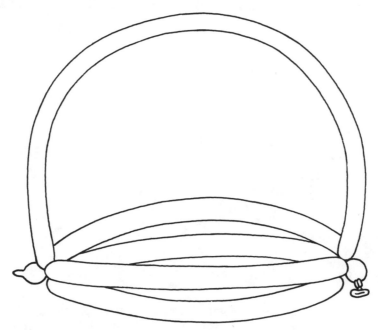

Figure 80

Adjust the tubes so the basket sits on the table by itself. You may have to turn a tube here and there to do this.

Bananas

Naturally, you will use a regular size yellow balloon for your bunch of Bananas. Inflate the balloon so there is a one-inch tip. Let a small amount of air out and tie the knot. Find the midpoint of the balloon and give it a single twist at that point. Bring the two tubes together alongside one another. Twist them together at the center and give them a few turns (Figure 81A). Bring the knot end up to meet the twist at the top of the balloon. Twist the knot around the latex at the joint of the bubbles. Tuck it so

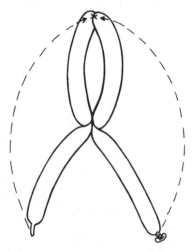

Figure 81 A

that it locks in place by itself. Now bring the tip end up and wrap it a few times around the knot end. Tuck in any loose piece. This is a bunch of four Bananas. Draw lines on the tubes and add a few dots to make it look more like a real bunch of fruit (Figure 81B).

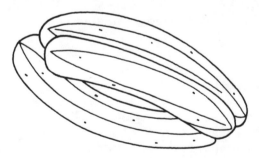

Figure 81 B

Apples

Use a yellow or green duo balloon for this sculpture. Inflate it so the balloon is only three inches long. Leave the colored tip free.

Tie the knot. You will be using the Apple Twist described in Chapter 2. Make the twist by inserting your right index finger in the knot end. Push the knot all the way through the inflated section into the colored end of the balloon. Your left fingers should grip the knot through the latex. Gently remove your index finger. Hold the knot firmly and twist the body of the balloon for at least a dozen turns. Set the balloon on a table and voila! An Apple! You may wish to make two or three in various colors for your basket.

For a place card, you might try making the Apple and set a drinking straw in the bottom hole (Figure 82). Place it in an empty

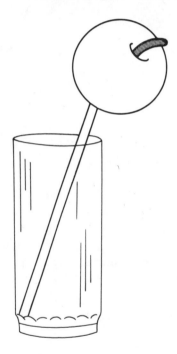

Figure 82

drinking glass in front of each child's place at the table. Write the child's name on the Apple with a marking pen.

If you wish more realistic apples, balloon dealers sell "Apple" balloons in various colors that have rounded rather than pointed tips.

Oranges, Lemons, Limes

The fruits in this series depend on the color you use. I suggest using an orange duo balloon for Oranges, yellow for Lemons, and green for Limes. This is now to make Oranges. Inflate the duo balloon until it is two inches long. Tie the knot. Now tie another knot at the point where the tip meets the inflated end. Stretch the latex so you can make a regular knot (Figure 83).

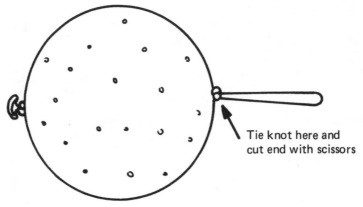

Tie knot here and cut end with scissors

Figure 83

Cut off the loose tip with sharp scissors. Be careful not to cut into the knot, or you will deflate the balloon. Decorate the Oranges with black or green dots to simulate imperfections on an orange.

Lemons and Limes are made exactly the same way. Just use about an inch and a half for the initial, inflated section.

Grapes, Cherries

Choose regular, red pencil balloons for your Cherries, green or blue for Grapes. Inflate the balloon halfway, as you did for Mouse in Chapter 4. Begin by twisting one-inch bubbles as if you were making the Mouse. Lock every third bubble as you did the Mouse's nose and ears. Twist to lock. Make as many small bubbles as you can. Lock every third one until you run out of air. You will end up with a tiny tail. Tuck the tail into the small bunch of bubbles and wrap it around the bubbles a few times to hide it. I suggest making two or three bunches for your basket (Figure 84).

Figure 84

Filling the Fruit Basket

Assemble all the fruits you have made. A good selection might include a bunch of Bananas, two bunches of Grapes or Cherries, two

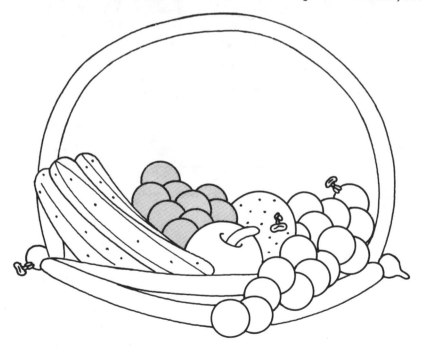

Figure 85

Apples, a Lime, and an Orange. You will need a small bottle of rubber cement. Don't brush cement on your balloon, or it will break. Merely dab your finger in the cement and touch a spot on the basket where you wish to glue a piece of fruit. A single dab of cement will lock the fruit in place. Add the fruit to the basket, one piece at a time. The Bananas may be on one side and the Grapes on the other, with the larger pieces in the center of the basket. Use your artistic talents to balance the colors and the design (Figure 85).

Balloon Bow

The Balloon Bow is great for the Fruit Basket. It also serves as a wrapping for baskets or for decorating soda bottles on your table. Blow up a regular red or pink pencil balloon, leaving about six inches for the tip (less if you wish a larger bow). Tie a knot at the tip. Find the halfway point in the tube and twist a single turn at that point.

Tie the loose end to the knotted end as you did in making the cradle of the basket. Now twist a figure eight by pressing the tied end to the twisted end. Give the balloon a few twists at this point (Figure 86). To release the air, cut the tip of the loose tail

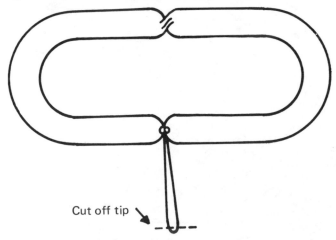

Cut off tip

Figure 86

at the very end. You can use this to tie your balloon to the handle of the basket. Merely wrap it around the handle and twist it a few times around the bow.

If you wish to use the bow elsewhere, cut off the extra tail. Use an uninflated balloon as a string to tie the bow to your package or bottle. Balloons will occasionally break. Save the broken long ends to use in place of string for the bows or instead of the rubber band around the neck of Dobbin the Horse.

Balloon Flowers

A few Balloon Flowers in a vase or large soda glass will add color to a table or a room. Inflate a long pencil balloon, leaving a three-inch tail. Let out a small amount of air and tie off the balloon. Poke your right index finger into the knot end so that it extends through the center about an inch and a half. With your left fingers,

Figure 87

grip the knot from outside the balloon. Make an Apple Twist by removing your index finger gently and twisting the small bubble several times to lock it in place.

Measure a section about two and a half inches from the bubble you just formed. Fold the balloon over so that it rests alongside the two-and-a half-inch section. Use a Quick-Lock Twist to form the two tubes into a loop. Lock the loop by twisting it around the small Apple-Twist bubble. Repeat this procedure with another two-and-a-half-inch section. Fold it and Quick-Lock Twist another loop. One more loop locked into the small bubble gives you three petals and a center bubble bud for your flower. The remainder of the balloon serves as the stem (Figure 87). If you puncture a small hole in the tip you can cement the flower to your fruit basket in place of the bow. It also makes a nice place card when set in a drinking glass in front of the table setting. Write your guest's name on the stem with a felt marking pen.

Tulips

Use one of each of the different colored balloons for a display of tulips. This is how to make each one. Inflate a regular balloon to

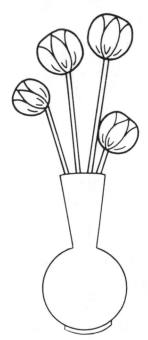

Figure 88

about three inches. Tie it off and poke your index finger into the knot end. Catch this piece with your left fingers and make an Apple Twist. This gives you an extra-long stem—perfect for placing in a small bud vase. Draw a few petal shapes on the bubble. Do this with as many balloons as will fit in the neck of the vase (Figure 88).

Balloon Hats

You can have a lot of fun at home or at parties making and wearing balloon sculptures as hats. One such hat is the Swan, which can be made and placed on your head for a fast laugh. Other animals can be worn by attaching them to a circle or a base such as we use in balloon displays. Here is a good basic form for almost any kind of hat.

Inflate a long pencil balloon as far as you can. Stretch it a bit as you blow it up. The tip should be as small as possible, no more than a quarter of an inch. Make a one-inch bubble at the knot end and twist it securely a few times. Do not let it go. Wrap the remainder of the balloon around the head of the person who will wear the hat. This will give you an idea of how large a circle you will need. Once you have determined the size of the ring needed, twist another bubble at that end (Figure 89). Lock the two end

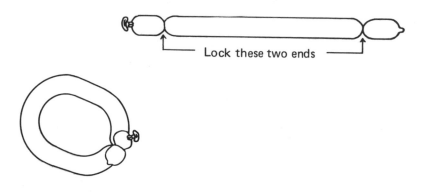

Lock these two ends

Figure 89

bubbles together. If you need a smaller hat, make the bubbles at the ends larger. You now have a ring to wear as a hat.

Inflate another regular-size balloon, allowing about half an inch for the tip. Make a two-inch bubble at the knot end and twist this section into the bubble end of the hat ring. The result is a hat with a large feather-like tube sticking up in front (Figure 90). If you decorate this with colored marking pens, as an Indian

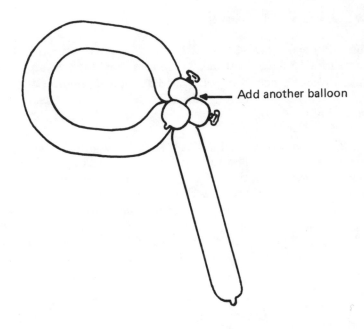

Add another balloon

Figure 90

feather, it can be worn with the long section at the back of the head. If you wear the long tube in front of your head, decorate it as a sultan's hat with a feather and a jewel design in front (Figure 91).

Turn the ring upside down and wear it with the long tube hanging down toward your back. Decorate this construction to look like a raccoon's tail for your Davy Crockett hat. Pull it around to the front, and it will look like an elephant's trunk.

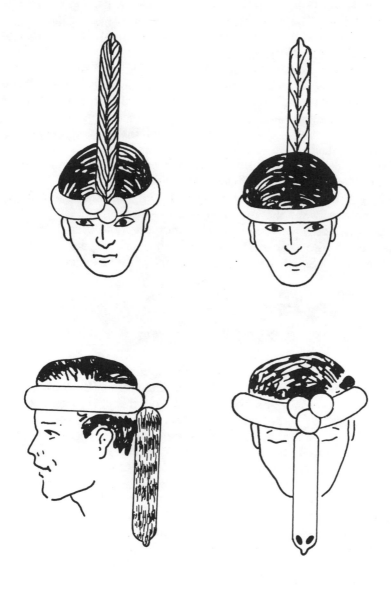

Figure 91

This is a versatile hat. If you bring the tip to the center of the balloon and wrap or tie it around in front, you have a hat with a top. This would be a good place to add a bunch of bananas or an apple, for a comical fruit hat.

A base for displaying balloon animals can also serve as a nice hat. Inflate the balloon, leaving a half-inch tip. Find the halfway point, as you did with the base of Dobbin the Horse. Twist it into two adjacent tubes. Tie the knot end to the tip end. Quick-Lock Twist the tied ends to form two small bubbles. This hat can be worn by itself . . . but add a few simple animals, such as a mouse or a dog, and you have cute fun hats. A flower added to one of the basic styles also makes a fun hat.

Attach these animals by using a dab of rubber cement at the base where you want the animal to sit.

Design your own hats with rings and bubbles added or twisted in. Make a Fruit Basket without a handle, add the fruit, and wear it as a South American fiesta hat. Use your imagination!

Displaying Balloon Sculptures

Many of your animals and shapes will stand by themselves. The Swan, Rabbit, and Dobbin the Horse can sit on the table alone. Others can be set in the tops of soda bottles. To attach them, use a small bit of clear-plastic cellophane tape. The best glue for balloons is a clear rubber cement. A small dab is sufficient.

Make a small display stand by inflating a regular pencil balloon, leaving a quarter-inch tip. Twist the balloon at the center as you did for the base of the Fruit Basket. This gives you two tubes alongside one another. Tie the knot end to the tip. You may have to stretch the tip somewhat to make it long enough to tie. This stand is ideal for displaying any animals you make. Merely dab some rubber cement on your finger and touch it to the parts of the animal you wish to attach to the stand (see Figure 49).

You can hang many of your sculptures in a doorway or from a light fixture. Tie them gently with a thin circle of string. Because balloons are lightweight, a thin string will carry them nicely. Do not allow the string to put any pressure on the tubes. Bumble-bees and Hummingbirds make good hanging displays, as does your attractive Octopus.

Chapter 7

Drawing Faces and Highlights

While all the animals we have made can be recognized easily, a few lines with a felt marking pen greatly enhance the sculpture. Two circles for eyes, or perhaps a line at the mouth for a smile, will make your balloon sculpture much more pleasant. For example, lines on the body can represent wings on the Swan. A few irregular circles on the Giraffe's body will make it more realistic.

The best way to draw on a soft balloon is with a felt-tip marking pen. Not all pens will work. Here are some names and makers of pens that do write on balloons: Marks-a-Lot (Carter), El Marko (Flair), Hi-Impact (Sanford), and Sharpie (Sanford). They are quick drying felt pens that produce clear, permanent lines. Other pens may work also, so you must experiment. Make sure they dry quickly and do not smudge or rub off once the ink is dried.

The best color to use is black, as it is highly visible from a distance. If you want more color for your party designs, add reds, blues, greens, etc. Allow the marker to ride the surface on the balloon. Do not exert pressure, or you might burst the balloon.

Bursting happens not so much from pressure but, often, from chemicals in the ink. A simple, fine line or circle is all you need. You don't have to be a great artist to make your balloons interest-

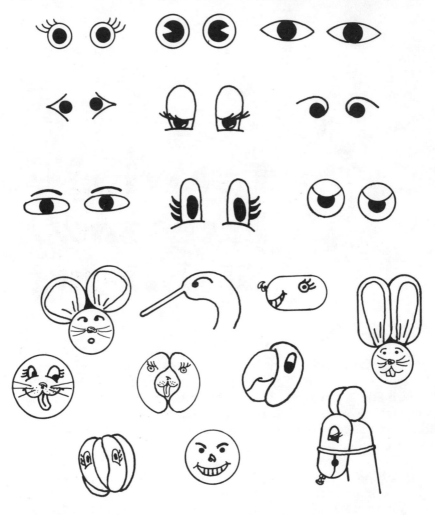

Figure 92

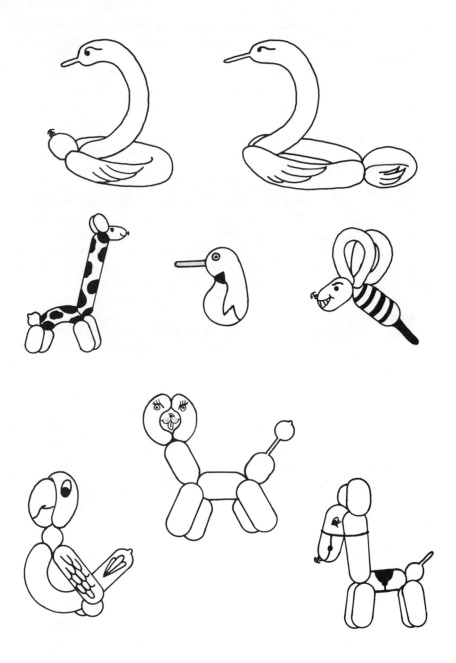

Figure 93

ing. Your animals can be comical or not, depending on your drawing. In Figure 92 are some shapes you might want to consider
as highlights.

Try to make your animals lifelike. For example, to create
the Giraffe's spotted look, you need irregular circles on its neck
and back. Your Swan is quite graceful and should have a delicate,
thin eye. To be in character, the Poodle could use eyelashes
around its eyes. Eyeglasses give an animal a comical appearance.
The Penguin, in its "tuxedo," needs a line of demarcation between
the front and back of its body. A bow tie under its chin might be
funny (Figure 93).

Personalizing the animals always makes a big hit at children's
parties. Write the child's name on an animal. Write or print
clearly on the largest surface of the figure. "Happy Birthday," or
"Get Well Soon" drawn on the handle of a Fruit Basket makes
your sculpture both a greeting card and a gift. I suggest adding
the children's names to the party hats you'll make for them.
That will keep the youngsters from arguing about whose animal
is whose.

Joe La Monica describes an alphabet that can be learned in
a few minutes. The description appears in volume 2 of his book
on balloon sculptures.

Chapter 8

Games
with
Balloons

Party games can be extra fun when pencil balloons are used as part of the games.

Long Shot

Here is a game called "Long Shot." Any number of people can play. You must have a different color balloon for each player. If there are more players than colors, write a name or number on the balloon so it can be identified with its owner. Inflate extralong balloons so they are all the same length. Leave the smallest tip possible.

Each player must shoot a balloon across the room. The balloon should be held firmly between the thumb and middle finger. The index finger is pushed from the knot end into the balloon as far as it will go. Each player is allowed to extend his or her arm out in front and release the balloon by relaxing the fingers. The balloon will fly straight ahead, up into the air or off to the side, depending on the wind, room temperature, air conditioning, etc. The player whose balloon travels the farthest is the winner.

The game is a lot of fun, because the balloons cannot be controlled accurately. It is easy to play, and no one can get hurt. Just be sure that no lightweight, breakable objects are in the path of the balloons. After you have played the game a few times, you can turn the balloons into simple hats. Fold a balloon in half and Quick-Lock Twist two bubbles at the tie end. Lock it in place and put the ring on your head. The result is a funny hat.

William Tell

The game of William Tell was originated as a bit by Jack Rosa, who used it in his hilarious children's show. You will need two people. One person portrays William Tell; the other plays his son.

William Tell, using a bow and arrow, shot an apple off the

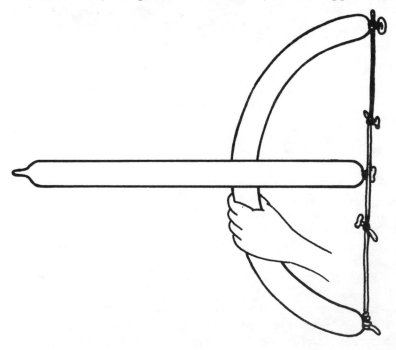

Figure 94

head of his son. In this game, the players re-create the scene, using balloon props.

Use a long pencil balloon for the bow. Inflate it, leaving a half-inch tip. Tie it off securely. Now tie together three regular, uninflated pencil balloons, end over end, so you get a long chain. Tie one end of the chain to the long balloon at the knot end; tie the other end to the knot. This gives you a bow (Figure 94). Inflate another long balloon as straight as possible, leaving a small tip. This is your arrow. Have someone hold the bow lightly in the center with the left hand. This player should place the loose balloon across the bow so the knot end is at the bowstring, with the tip pointing ahead and resting on the player's left hand. Allow "William Tell" to pull back the string, at the same time inserting his right index finger in the knot of the loose balloon. When he lets go, the balloon will fly out as in the Long Shot game.

Make a large Apple from a duo balloon and place it on top of the second player's head. The object of the game is for William Tell to shoot the Apple off the second player's head. It is very difficult to do, so allow the player three tries. At the same time, the second player must try to keep the Apple balanced on top of his head. If he moves, the Apple will fall and the player loses.

Into the Loop

In this game each player shoots a rocket into a large, hanging loop. Each time a player is successful, points are awarded. The first one to reach a given number of points wins the game. The rules are decided on before the game, so there will be no misunderstanding later.

You will need a large pencil balloon blown as long as you can get it. Leave a quarter-inch tip so it can be tied to the knot after you have inflated it. Hang this circle in the doorway. As in the other games, the rockets or arrows are shot from a given distance by inserting the index finger in the knot end of the balloon.

Chapter 9

Tips–
Patter–
Bits

The following suggestions are made to help you increase your success in your newly learned art of balloon sculpture.

* *Care of Your Hands*
  It is important for you to take good care of your hands if you expect to make balloon animals. Rough skin or sharp fingernails will defeat your efforts every time. Keep your hands clean and your nails trimmed and filed.

* *Courtesy*
  As you work with balloons, onlookers are bound to ask you the same questions over and over again. *Never be rude or annoyed.* Since they are asking questions, they are impressed and would like to know more about what you are doing. You will increase the pleasure if you keep a sense of humor. People will ask, "Do they break

often?'' A good answer is "No. They break only once.''
"How long have you been doing this?'' You may reply,
"Since I got here this afternoon.'' "Does it take a lot of
practice?'' Your answer, "No. Just a lot of hot air.''

* *Have Fun*
If you are planning to entertain with your art, do so. Be
pleasant and have fun yourself. Here are some bits that
will always get laughs from small children.

* *Bits*
Before starting to inflate a balloon, hold it to your lips
and stretch the latex as far as it will go. Release the end
and allow it to snap back so that it hits the palm of your
hand. The balloon acts like a rubber band. After the
snap, rub your nose and say "Ouch!'' The children will
think that's very funny.

Blow up a duo balloon, but do not tie it. Instead, let the
air out so that it blows back and cools your face. Say,
"It's really hot in here. That's so much better.''

Here is another cute bit of business you might try. Inflate a pencil balloon and tie it off. Find the exact center
and twist the balloon at that point, making two long
bubbles. Hold the bubbles, one in each hand. Your
thumbs should meet at the twisted section. Stretch the
twisted section by pulling your hands apart. This breaks
the balloon in half, but the air will be locked between
your thumbs and index fingers. Offer a half to two
spectators. As they reach for the balloons, relax the
pressure of your thumbs, and the balloons will fly away.

* *Cellosticks*
Professional balloon workers use Cellosticks to display
their models. These are long, waxed sticks. They fit into
the twists and are used to mount the designs or to offer
them to children to carry away. The sticks are sold by
some professional balloon dealers.

Where to Buy Balloons

The first place to look for replacement balloons is in the store where you bought this book. Such stores sell packages of the three standard sizes used for all the models described here. If your store doesn't carry them, look in the phone book for the name of a magic trick shop in your area. They carry entertainer pencil balloons in the same sizes in addition to other useful items. If you wish to get price and accessory lists, write to some pro shops. Always include a stamped self-addressed envelope for the reply. Write to:

> Jack Rosa Balloons
> 457 Ball Court
> Kissimee
> Florida 32741
>
> or
>
> Show-Biz Services
> 1735 East 26th Street
> Brooklyn
> New York 11229

Both suppliers do business by mail only. They will supply balloon books, pumps, and other accessories.

Using Your New Skills

Once you have mastered the craft of balloon modeling, you can use your skill to earn extra money. Begin by offering your services free of charge to charity groups such as churches, senior citizens clubs, and day-care centers. You will soon develop a routine and learn to make the animals under the pressure of being watched as you work. If you're good, people will ask you to do other things, for example, birthday parties, for which you can charge a fee.

Once you have done a few free shows, you are ready to offer your talent to local restaurants that book children's parties and that often hire a balloon worker for Sunday brunches or weekend walk-arounds. You may find that wearing a clown costume will get you more of this type of work. Contact some party planners in the phone book and tell them about yourself and your skills. They are always looking for people to do decorations, and you can be added to their list of party entertainers.

If you are really interested in earning money at this hobby, you will want to get more information on advanced sculpting and other sculptures. See the bibliography in the back of this book for a list of the better books on the subject. Professional balloon suppliers and magic shops carry these books in stock. Good luck!

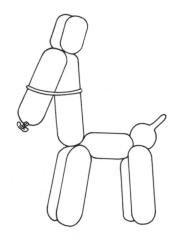

Bibliography

Andrews, Val. *Manual of Balloon Modeling.* New York: Magico, 1981.

Brearley, Doug. *All Wind & Twists.* Halifax, England: Playtime, 1973.

Davis, Jimmy. *One Balloon Zoo.* Chicago: Magic, Inc., 1966.

Dewey, Ralph. *Dewey's Basic Balloons.* Deer Park, Texas: Dewey, 1978.

La Monica, Joe. *La Monica's Balloon Sculpture.* New York: Special Arts, 1975.

Payne, James A. *Tiny's Balloon Animal Zoo.* Santa Cruz, Calif.: Tiny the Clown, 1980.

Sands, George. *Encyclopedic Balloon Modeling Course.* New York: Sands, 1971.

Siegel, Roger. *Rubber Ark.* Chicago: Magic, Inc., 1971.

Index

Editorial and Graphic Services